Brushstrokes of the Mind

Also by Barbara Gurney and published by Ginninderra Press
Life's Shadows
Footprints of a Stranger
Purple and Other Hues
Seeking Self

Barbara Gurney

Brushstrokes of the Mind

Brushstrokes of the Mind
ISBN 978 1 76109 575 7
Copyright © Barbara Gurney 2023

First published 2023 by
GINNINDERRA PRESS
PO Box 3461 Port Adelaide 5015
www.ginninderrapress.com.au

Contents

Feathering	7
Lisa's Worth	8
Mellow Glow	10
Doves	11
Mary Carroll Park	12
Malevolence	13
Roses of the Heart	14
Deceit of Beauty	15
Speck of Quiet	16
Seaside Ditty	17
Newspaper	18
Sparkle	19
Sand Between My Toes	20
Veil of Change	21
Mysticism of Mornings	22
Beyond Hate	23
Pledged	24
It's Only a Spider!	25
Conviction	26
Finishing Touch	27
Black and White	28
Mere Jolt	29
Revisiting Rejection	30
Kindness Goes a Long Way	31
Where is Home	32
Processing	33
One Bullet is Too Many	34
Apart	35
Hello	36
It Will Surely Pass	37

Futile Reflection	38
Across Deep Water	39
Nature Repairs	40
They Stand	41
Like Dust	42
Knowing	43
Dance	44
Footprints On My Heart	45
Gold	46
Colour Me	47
Advantage of Time	48
A Moment of Hesitation	49
City Burns	50
Hidden Picture	51
Clasp My Heart	52
Eyes	53
City Warrior	54
Beautiful Difference	55
Let Your Children Go…	56
Rainbow Gold	57
Nothing/Everything	58
Desire	59
Touch	60
Ants	61
The Tangle of Learning	62
Destruction of Art	63
Uncharted	64
Dad	65
Miracles in the Sand	66
Questions and Answers	67
Emotional Feet	68
Scraps	69

Feathering

A kind word,

      like a feather touching lightly on a pond,

is something beautiful.

Lisa's Worth

You can't,
    can't
        can't
You're no good
    no good
        no good

Words that nibble at confidence
Words that swallow accolades:
    compliments
    promotions
    honours

Huddled in a cocoon of doubt, Lisa succumbs to the dire predictions
There's no escaping the tentacles of rejection
There's no escaping the tentacles of dejection

She is all she's been told
She is all of those expectations

Lisa's shoulders droop
The tightness in her throat, keeps the bile at bay

She reaches for the compensation of praise
She reaches for the compensation of acknowledgement
    well done
    fabulous
    believe in yourself

Her nook of comfort zone wraps around hope,
but loosens as *no good* screams again.
She only believes in *can't*

Why is Lisa's worth enclosed in a few malicious words
Words which have so much power
Words which shouldn't have so much power

Please, Lisa
Cast them away
Be done with them
You can
      can
            can

Mellow Glow

Across oceans my thoughts wander:

>To a time amongst distant towns
>when awe and grandeur gripped our hearts
>the unfamiliar of ancient buildings
>eased into a welcoming form
>
>To sun-filled moments on shoreline walks
>when footprints formed on pebbly beaches
>the brilliant hue of seaside waves
>eased into shallow wash
>
>To days slipping into evening splendour
>when time ensured our memories stay
>the hushed tones of softer nights
>eased into a mellow glow

Doves

If I could fly
    doves would be my flock
I'd beg their wings could beat so strong
    and swarm to far off lands
cover dejected shoulders
    with feathers of empathy and love
coo with a song of hope
    to those who've lost their future
strut with confidence
    alongside the downcast and joyless
perch on graves of the brave
    carry their soul to infinity

If only I could fly

Mary Carroll Park

Beside the toil of man
Where bitumen takes us away
A jewel
An oasis
Of sounds and splendid vistas
Bidding us stay a while
In nature
In a capsule of time
Explore
Absorb
Nesting swans, ducklings, turtles
Squabbling twenty-eights and pretty galahs
Delighting us
Filling us with joy

Malevolence

Across the powdery sand
Tiptoes of waves wander
Lacey edges dance to their destination
Returning to enticing depths
Tempting the naïve

Lurking beneath the shimmering surface
Invisible danger loiters
Steadfast stealth with razor teeth
Or wisps of poisonous tentacles
With their own agenda

Sparkling blueness beckons
Doubtful delight in this wondrous ocean

Roses of the Heart

My mum loved yellow roses
Me?
Pink ones are my favourites

Be it one colour or the other
Each delicate petal clings to a memory:
      the sweet perfume of home
      the thorn of tough teachings
      the sprouting leaves of essential growth

Yellow?
Pink?

All rose blossoms speak of
      yesterday
      comfort
      love

Deceit of Beauty

Age defied in the lens
A tilt of elegance
Dark lashes entice desire

Beneath are lies

Look upon the loveliness with sadness
Have mercy for this beautiful shell
For the inner soul is broken

Speck of Quiet

The numbness of silence
>between
>>the shock of hearing
>>>and the awful knowledge of believing

Seaside Ditty

The chilly ocean holds no fear
For granny May and friends so dear

They dip their feet in water deep
Secrets old are safe to keep

Life may bring them aches and pain
But beachside frolics are all about gain

Coffee, cake and complaints go down
After the swim without a frown

In sunshine, rain, they're out to play
Bringing the thrill of each new day

They are blessed, that is for sure
With sunshine, laughs and so much more

Newspaper

I feel…
    like a piece of newspaper
    clipped for its importance
    discarded when the moment passes

Sparkle

I break free

       from the restraint of the reserved
       from the agony of the ordinary
       from the torment of the trite

prepared to shine

Sand Between My Toes

In the misty morning I step into another world
    sand between my toes
        hair slapping against my face
        eyes squinting into the breeze

I wrap my scarf tighter
tuck shivering hands deep into pockets

Gone are the begging pressures of time
The listed chores on a notepad – forgotten
    ironing, vacuuming, dusting, cooking, weeding
        earning, facilitating, managing, controlling, doing

With sand on my feet
and wind at my face
in this luxury of nature
I lose the me others need
I become the me I need to be

Veil of Change

Declare love
Despite anguish
Of belligerent opposition

Defy the failure
Of those under beating sun
That falls on all lands

Understand
Waves touch each shore
Of blameless oceans

Break boundaries of heritage
Take your oath
Under a veil of change

Mysticism of Mornings

A surrounding essence of pleasure
Like waves caressing the sand
Bubbling on contact
An ecstasy to share
Sighing on retreat
Content with the calm

Life skips
Life whistles
Life smiles

Beyond Hate

I am Lucifer
– powerful with the fire of hate

flames of malice consume happiness
sucks oxygen from joy

souls buckle

I dance in celebration
laughter bursts from my malevolent lungs
sprouts evil
I fan the embers of wickedness

the souls, smothered with cinders, gather courage

I slip on their daring
hope drapes heavy over my back
I fall
their inferno of determination devours me

tears from loved ones fall onto this hell
drowns the blaze
cleanses them
washes me away

Pledged

My lover's breath touches my cheek
His kiss promises delight
Yellow and burning orange shout from the horizon
Creating memories for our tomorrows
Banded with gold
Pledged until old

It's Only a Spider!

The silver strands declare it's there
A home strung between the leaves
It sways ever so gently
with the breeze or passersby

Raindrops hang like twinkling jewels
Upon silken threads
Sunshine makes a rainbow
Despite the deadly trap

It devours those caught
A meal complete
An unsuspecting living creature
Glued to this web of death

The spider's home can be fragile
Sticky and strong besides
Splendour that's admired by many
Killed by an ignorant few

The beauty of a tangled web
In which he weaves his prey
Can be destroyed by man
In a single stroke of fear

Man shouldn't claim abhorrence
The spider has a right to life
It's a part of the chain in nature
Each valuable and must remain

Conviction

Emotions strong
Heartbeat rising
Sweat on brow
Placards raised

We need these folk of conviction
These people with challenging views

There'd be no vote for women
No say in what they felt
There'd be no sootless workplace
No fairness on the factory floor

There'd be no bus or trains or planes
If inventions were ignored
There'd be no medical advancement
If defiant risks went unheeded

Emotions strong
Heart beat rising
Sweat on brow
Forging forward

We need these folks of courage
These people of conviction

Finishing Touch

Life needs cherries
A cherry to top it all off
A cherry as the finishing touch

Amongst the days of busyness
Of angst and anxiety

When smiles are welcome
And hugs are needed

Life needs cherries
A cherry to top it all off
A cherry as the finishing touch

Black and White

Look closely
Do you see my worth?

Not in the sketch of my appearance
But in the detail

Come closer
See my faults and failings
My positives and potential
See beyond the plain into the intricate
My nooks and crannies of personality
Where I hide pain, hold joy
Amongst desires and despair
This is where I truly am

Mere Jolt

This motionless is not the stillness of peace
I sit, bereft of any desire to continue
Lost in the inability to find momentum

It took a mere jolt of a moment – and you were gone
No longer a part of my anything
Left only a handful of yesterdays

Revisiting Rejection

The hurt hides
Down in the depths of hunger for acceptance

Long, long ago the whispers of adolescence sprouted
    where skipping
    and giggling
    and irresponsibility
    were heralded with the exuberance of naivety

Then rejection slapped like a sword against armour
Denting this energy for life
breaking the bond of a developing closeness
    where smiling
    and sharing
    and loving
    were shattered on the path to adulthood

time passes and memories appear
    where youth is recollected
    and rehashed
    and the hurt of rejection revisits

Kindness Goes a Long Way

Blackened by the everyday
Each piece holding together – just

Burnt with failure
Scored by ingrained doubt

Be kind to one another

The person who locks away their feelings
– seeing through blemished eyes
Might need the flame of hurt extinguished
Might want a soothing touch

Be kind to one another

One who reaches beyond broken promises
– struggling with dented confidence
Might need a tender embrace
Might want a simple smile

Be kind to one another

Where is Home

Ukraine invasion – March 2022

Beneath rubble of atrocity
Under broken dreams and loss of hope
Below broken cups and shreds of photographs
Is a home that is no more

Frightened children cry soft and long
Aware all they have is now
A hand to hold, a breath to take
A safe haven no longer their home

Heartbroken souls weep in vain
Their life cruelly snatched away
One step further and another
To a land they can not claim

Lines of human misery grasp escape
Past tanks and threatening enemy
No food, no clothes, no comfort
Nothing but continuing despair

They trudge away from war
Towards empathy of strangers
To new of place, of new beginnings
But, you ask, where is home

Processing

Delicately she waits
With downcast eyes
Honouring the process

But what if…

The geisha knows her value
Living two lives
Pocketing success
Waiting for opportunity
To declare supremacy

Just hidden behind the process

One Bullet is Too Many

Only one bullet
Breaks the innocence of schoolchildren
How many must we abide

Overlapping confusion
Feet screaming toward safety
Hands running away from fear

Motionless bodies
Unable to learn
Anymore

Apart

I dream of snow-covered cobblestones
of towering spires
where far away under Christmas lights
traditions are different but mean the same

Gifts are given
        but I'm not there
Glasses are raised
        that I can't share

So while we linger beside our tree
My heart is here
but it is there
Torn with separation
Saved by love

Hello

Hello
It's me
>struggling

See,
it's me
>battling

But…

The depths of imagination
>delivers me
>from myself
>takes me into tomorrow

It Will Surely Pass

From horizontal pose
Amid green of grass
Near red of brick
The world is blue
Clear
Crisp
Blue neighbouring blue
A calming blue
Not the named blues of lost hope

Hues, impossible to duplicate, slowly descend
Gathers the skirt of concealment beyond rays of sun
Indigo sips into inky black – stealing yesternight
The evening star sprinkles the expectation of past forevers
And the moon smiles – declares another day will be

Futile Reflection

Fire spreads without care
Refusing to surrender the torture
Advancing, hesitating, advancing
      – dancing through landscapes
Tormenting with its own beauty
Clashing the brilliance of flames to the darkness of destruction

We can but stand
Without colour
Bland and ineffective
Bringing contrast like a futile reflection

Across Deep Water

Far across deep water
    Where whales emit their breath
    Travelling to home and birth
    Where waves toss
    And seaweed gathers against pebbled soil and cliff-faced barriers

Far across ancient lands
    Where armies trod on foreign soil
    Of battles toiled – most times lost
    Where brave souls survived and carried on

Far across the streets of Prague
    Where bridges span the mighty Vltava
    Where spires reach into snowy skies
    And cobblestones forget my tread

There's a little boy in man-filled shoes
Tendering his own offspring
Reminding my heart of long-ago times
When he was young
And I was too

Nature Repairs

In the stillness of a misty morn
Icy fingers of autumn dew
Touches delicate growth
Struggling for survival

> Cymbals of pain CRASH
> A trumpet of agony BLARES
> The march across sensitive human nerves begins
>
> Amid tuneless cries for help
> Tentacles of relief strangle the band of suffering
> Finally beating a fanfare on retreat

The morning mist lifts
And nature repairs itself

They Stand

They stand
Solid in their connection
Rooted with the beginning of earth
When footsteps were few
    Wildlife foraged
    Swans flew
When ripples turned to rage and smashed upon sandy pockets

Dawn creates mist-settling scenes
Grasses accepts the wrap of drama
Enchantment wafts and the river basks in the early morning atmosphere

These majestic trees of countless hues and touch
    Silver and smooth
    Rough and scarred
Each a monument
With beauty a force
Enduring man and beast

The calm of past days swallowed by progress
Man spins wheels along shared paths
Concrete weaves for easy tread
Brick walls contain the water's journey

But still they stand
Branches reaching over the busyness
Shading the human longing for togetherness
Displaying the comfort of nature

Determined to grace every eventuality
They stand defiant

Like Dust

Dust, blown by a malicious wind, carelessly dropping particles
on the unsuspecting landscape
> *like*
>> whispers of hate across pages on the internet

Taunting as the beastly breeze wans, lingers, then settles
Building patterns on lush green growth between bounty and destruction
> *like*
>> impressionable youth, yet to know boundaries.
>> struggling for the fortitude against comparison and temptation

Knowing

The knowing of you was like an unexpected rainbow
The loss of this knowing unravelled my life

My past perceptions battered by your fists
Love torn from me, landing on the floor with my shirt

Scars deeper than the one on my cheek
Unseen bruises throb in time with dread

Fear exploded through my veins at your voice
Is there nowhere to hide except in cowering?

The knowing of you was like a sparkling diamond
The loss of this knowing collapsed my world

Dance

Black and grey and every other shade of…
    between

Life rains down many struggles
Enough to cover joy with clouds
Throw lightning at happiness
Drown out pleasure with thunder

The storm of the day will surely pass
Grab your version of sunshine and…
    dance

Footprints On My Heart

This ache is heavy on my heart
There's longing and desire
For things and those long missed
For forgotten days gone by

I sit and watch the clouds
Dance across a brilliant sky
They leave me here alone
To think upon my youth

The ebb and flow of emotion
Like waves upon my soul
Brings longing like a storm
And challenges the mind

Flashes of memorable moments
Charge through my wandering thoughts
I sigh and wipe a tear away
And ponder love long lost

The gentle smile of one that's dear
An embrace from one that's close
Footprints upon my heart remain
All else has passed away

Gold

The blue clings
But I'm determined to be free

I will emerge to the world
Put on a face of glee
Show the appearance of delight
Go forward until I shine
Declaring contentment and bliss

Turn the blue to gold

Colour Me

My soul relinquishes discontent
        the lurking darkness
        the lack-lustre mindset
        the grey and gloomy mist of misery

I desire shades of enchantment
        the bliss of a new day
        the merriment of friends
        the pleasure of coffee and cake

Colour me the red of vitality
Colour me the yellow of delight
Colour me the blue of contentment

Let colour wrap me afresh

Advantage of Time

Can the effects of time
        shine an advantage
        soften the disappearance of youth
        mellow the urgent struggle of middle years

Is the me of older years
        a gentler soul
        with a spark igniting a warming glow
        without the fierceness of burning flames

If who I was is gone
        do I question the me I've become
        or simply accept a me of now

A Moment of Hesitation

Upon green fields I gaze
The flush of autumn bidding me welcome
>   *I pause*

The mountain protects
A valley full of family
>   *I pause*

Moving on, memories return
The homestead a childhood sanctuary
>   *I pause*

So long has been my sojourn
Will all be the same
>   *I pause*

I draw closer, my footsteps quicken
Echoing the beat of my heart
>   *I pause*

The door opens
Arms of embrace extend to me
>   *I no longer pause*

City Burns

The city burns while souls sleep

Flames consume with reddish delight:
    filing cabinets
    white-collared desks

Crows flap above lost success.
Homeless shapes shuffle from alleys, dragging hopelessness

Sirens screech:
    Warning the innocent
    Damning the arsonists

The horizon reflects the burning and ash will own tomorrow

Hidden Picture

There is a picture on my wall that hides my heart
Tall steeples stretch skywards like arms reaching for love
The cobblestones remind me of echoing footsteps trod with a
 small hand in mine
Happy days spent beneath those blue skies twinkle in the memory
The dark doorways of hidden pain allow sunshine to reach
 into corners

Clasp My Heart

New-born fingers wrapped around mine
I drifted to a place of joy
An aura of delight surrounded us
The symbol of this clasp became eternal

We crossed the road, hand in hand
On the way to unplanned adventures
Saw scurrying ants and squawking parrots
As two, we filled those hours

A full spectrum of emotions with fingers enlaced
Clenching for support when tears flowed
Lingering during occasions worth celebrating
Moments remembered throughout the years

A simple act of caring; no words needed
This hand-held bond grew firm
As you matured
And I grew old

And so,
As I prepare to leave you forever
Take my hand
And send me with love

Eyes

The eye to the soul is protected by the mind
but vision fades with consequences untimed

See flowers of gold and friends of old
Vistas of travel making memories to hold

Patterns of pleasure
and sparkles to treasure
Small things and large brought close without measure

Our eyes are taken for granted
until all are threatened

City Warrior

Bold like the colours of a city
Or is it
Monochrome
Isolating

Can one hide in buildings reaching the sky?

Can one still grow like a tree between concrete?

Time to challenge like an unfaltering warrior
Brave in attempting concepts anew
Brush aside notions of failure and pride
Press forward to new potentials

Beautiful Difference

The enfolds of society
        where customs hide
               in shadowy form

expose the traditions
        break down the barriers
               brighten the contrast

bond with the unknown
        welcome our differences
               share the beauty

Let Your Children Go…

Independence steals the joy of being needed

Teach them
Permit departure
Leaving all but the grip of belonging

Small remnants
Between their aspirations
Tokens of yesterday
When a mother's love was cleaved

Rainbow Gold

I never found the pot of gold
The one at the end of the rainbow

I reached out at the colours
towards:
>	The red; burning memories into forever
>	Orange – temptation
>	Yellow brighter than joy itself
>	Blessed blue
>	Calming green
>	with
>	indigo, darker than my darkest days
>	and
>	violet, hinting at something new

No, I never touched the rainbow
Never found that pot of gold

Far more precious
I found you
And accepted a band of gold

Nothing/Everything

It's not about me
But it's love that I need
Someone to understand
The fear of what's next

It's all about me
Pander my greed
For caring and nurture
Throughout my distress

It's not about you
But take my lead
I want your devotion
I have to confess

It's all about you
You should believe
Your total involvement
I ask nothing less

It's not about us
This we must heed
There're others who are hurting
But that's the test

It's all about us
Let's plant the seed
To honour the commitment
For we deserve best

Desire

I want to touch the texture of life amid calm or chaos
See splendour; let elegance drape across my skin

Be there – not here in the ordinary

I want to float around diamonds in inky skies
Grasp moonbeams; let them squiggle over my palms

Be there – not here in the ordinary

I want to float around tree tops of aromatic leaves
Grasp flowers; let them ooze scent on my fingers

Be there – not here in the ordinary

I want to float around tranquil water in aqua seas
Grasp seashells; let them forever be mine

Not here in the ordinary
I want to be there

Touch

Fingertips against cold steel
Palms pressed against bold surfaces
I need the knowledge of strength on my hands

Imagination's grand result
Moulded expression of talent
I need the pleasure of creation in my hands

I touch
I feel

Thank you

Ants

A straight line is the shortest distance between two points

One small ant can seem lost
Darting with anxious vigour
Making slow progress with frantic energy
Heedless of the distance travelled

When countless numbers clash
Chaos reigns supreme
They muddle through the journey
Reaching a consensus of misunderstanding

They scurry on their frenzied way
Detouring in circles
Running this way and back
With boundless enthusiasm or confused tracking

It is obvious ants have never attended geometry class

The Tangle of Learning

We need more than ABC
We need nurture and caring

Colour disappears from skin
When geography fades

Acknowledge history in its repeat
Understand the necessity for change

Soft words appease fury
Subtraction of anger a blessing

Learn these lessons
Reach out

Destruction of Art

From history we can but learn

When evil struck art perished
Jackboots stomped the ashes
Written word gone with intent

Old masters coveted by generals
Spirited away to salt mines
Awaiting possession for personal collections

Invasion trembled into peaceful streets
Revolutionaries tossed religious tomes into fire
Their way – the only way

Electronic acquisition unseen
Stolen by deliberate pirates
Shared without consent

Art exposure strangled by viruses
Absence of opportunity rampant
Creations stored away

Art is the essence of communities' soul
Lose the paint on canvas, pen on paper
Society will be blighted

Save our art

Uncharted

In the shadow of tomorrow
We stare into the beyond

Stories form from the unknown
Building myths and coining lies
Creating uncertainty and fear

Teachings change at discoveries anew
Challenging ancient theories
Rewriting guidelines and hypothesis

Money shouts to the stars
Desirous of reaching planets
Claiming success; explaining failures

In the shadow of tomorrow
We stare into the beyond
Contemplate possibilities

Dad

Huddled in my sorrow
I reach for your elusive shadow
Beyond the glue pot
Past the dovetail cuts

Your essence touches my DNA
Reflects in attitude
     – joy and despair

Haunted by the shortness of our time
But buoyed by precious memories

Miracles in the Sand

The water sits still
And the child? – Only for a moment

Movement catches her eye
She pokes and prods in a watery divot
Perhaps some miracle of nature will emerge
    – satisfy her curiosity

Her toes are covered with red, red mud
face splattered with freckles of spray
from when she jumped and shrieked
delighted with the impact her small self caused

This child won't be like the puddling left-over rain
sitting waiting to be absorbed by the elements
No!
She will race through life
examining every opportunity
stamping at humdrum
claiming her own miracles

Questions and Answers

Where is it going?
Why is it going?
Does it really matter?

Where are you going?
Why are you going?
Does it really matter?

As life presents a busy path
of trauma and pain
of tension and strain
Stand in the moment and reconsider

Footsteps taking you to knowledge
of perception and kindness
of fulfilment and calmness
Always matter

Emotional Feet

Our feet stand where they were when you left
The blossoms evoked spring – a time of fresh starts

And so it was with you
our daughter who sought space of proximity and emotion

Your adventure commenced at an airport
       continued in a country of White Christmases
       and distant cousins
Mail brought stories of visible breaths, short days
       and hot-bottle nights
          of underground railways and overhead vapour trails
          of saluting guardsmen and loud pipe bands
Our complaining hands held calendars as they flipped over,
  page after page

Then you wrote of thoughts of us
       of brittle wheat fields
       of Santa by the sea

Our feet stand where they were when you left
But this time, our arms are open as you walk towards us

Scraps

Reach for the ultimate sky
Stretch your gracefulness to the sun
Drip gorgeousness of wing
With fragility of design

As with nature
create exquisiteness of character

Take your scraps
Make glorious and shine

www.ingramcontent.com/pod-product-compliance
Lightning Source LLC
Chambersburg PA
CBHW071033080526
44587CB00015B/2600